COOL CARS

MCLAREN

BY DALTON RAINS

WWW.APEXEDITIONS.COM

Copyright © 2026 by Apex Editions, Mendota Heights, MN 55120. All rights reserved. No part of this book may be reproduced or utilized in any form or by any means without written permission from the publisher.

Apex is distributed by North Star Editions:
sales@northstareditions.com | 888-417-0195

Produced for Apex by Red Line Editorial.

Photographs ©: Pexels, cover; Shutterstock Images, 1, 4–5, 6–7, 9, 14, 16–17, 18, 19, 22–23, 26, 27, 29; Bernard Cahier/Hulton Archive/Getty Images, 10–11; Paul-Henri Cahier/Hulton Archive/Getty Images, 12–13; Joern Sackermann/Alamy, 21; Martyn Lucy/Getty Images Sport/Getty Images, 24–25

Library of Congress Control Number: 2025930301

ISBN
979-8-89250-524-6 (hardcover)
979-8-89250-560-4 (paperback)
979-8-89250-631-1 (ebook pdf)
979-8-89250-596-3 (hosted ebook)

Printed in the United States of America
Mankato, MN
082025

NOTE TO PARENTS AND EDUCATORS

Apex books are designed to build literacy skills in striving readers. Exciting, high-interest content attracts and holds readers' attention. The text is carefully leveled to allow students to achieve success quickly. Additional features, such as bolded glossary words for difficult terms, help build comprehension.

CHAPTER 1
FIRST-PLACE FINISH 4

CHAPTER 2
HISTORY 10

CHAPTER 3
SUPER SERIES 16

CHAPTER 4
ULTIMATE SERIES 22

COMPREHENSION QUESTIONS • 28
GLOSSARY • 30
TO LEARN MORE • 31
ABOUT THE AUTHOR • 31
INDEX • 32

CHAPTER 1

First-Place Finish

The 2024 Abu Dhabi **Grand Prix** begins. McLaren driver Lando Norris slams down on the gas. His **Formula 1** race car shoots forward.

Lando Norris races for McLaren during the 2024 Abu Dhabi Grand Prix.

McLaren's Formula 1 cars are bright orange. McLaren chose that color because it stands out on the track.

Norris veers around a tight turn. Then he speeds into the straightaway. Lap by lap, Norris grows his lead.

FAST FACT

Norris got his first Formula 1 win in 2024. Then he won three more races that year.

Norris stays in front from start to finish. His dominant race helps his team win the Constructor's Championship!

TOP TEAM

The 2024 title was McLaren's ninth Constructor's Championship. That honor goes to the team with the most points in a season. Teams get points when their drivers win races.

Norris (center) celebrates winning the 2024 Constructor's Championship with McLaren.

CHAPTER 2

History

McLaren started in 1963. It was founded by Bruce McLaren. The company's first Formula 1 car began racing in 1966.

Before founding his racing team, Bruce McLaren was a Formula 1 driver.

Bruce McLaren died in 1970. But the company continued on. McLaren won its first Constructor's Championship in 1974.

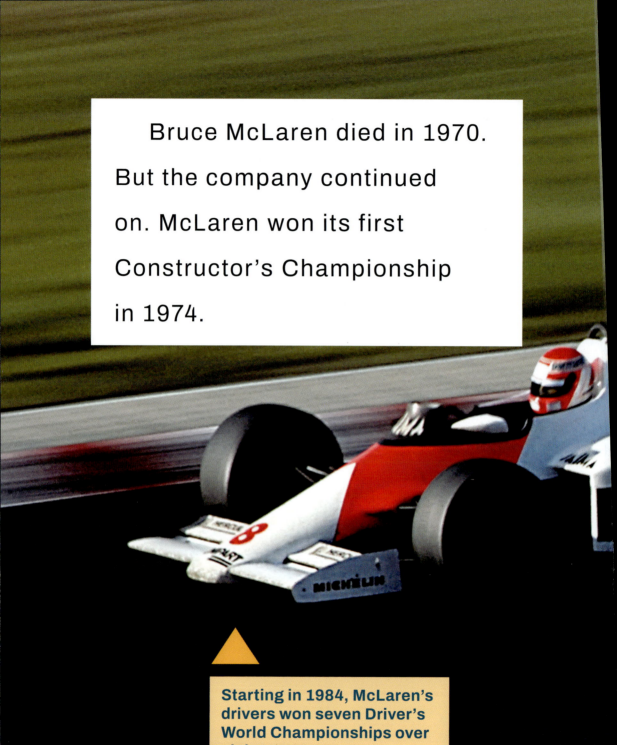

Starting in 1984, McLaren's drivers won seven Driver's World Championships over eight years.

NEW IDEAS

In 1981, the McLaren MP4/1 began racing. It was the first Formula 1 car made of carbon fiber. The material made the cars safer and quicker. Soon, all Formula 1 cars used carbon fiber.

Next, McLaren began making road-legal cars. The McLaren F1 first sold in 1992. It turned McLaren into a top sports car **brand**.

FAST FACT

The McLaren F1 set a speed record for road-legal cars. It hit 240.1 miles per hour (386.4 km/h).

◀ The McLaren F1 could reach 60 miles per hour (97 km/h) in 3.2 seconds.

CHAPTER 3

SUPER SERIES

By the 2020s, McLaren sold all kinds of sports cars. Some were part of the Super Series. The Artura was a **hybrid**. It had a low, sleek body.

Like McLaren's race cars, the Artura was made from carbon fiber.

The McLaren 750S was faster than the Artura. The car had hidden air **intakes**. They cooled the engine at high speeds. The smooth shape and large rear wing kept the 750S stable.

Drivers could choose convertible versions of the 750S or Artura.

The McLaren 765LT could hit 124 miles per hour (200 km/h) in just 7 seconds.

LIGHTWEIGHT LTS

The 765LT was made for track driving. McLaren **designed** lightweight wheels for the car. The car's new **exhausts** were lighter, too.

The McLaren GTS was made for road trips. It had a long body and lots of space inside. But the comfortable car was still fast.

FAST FACT

The GTS had a top speed of 203 miles per hour (326 km/h).

The GTS cost more than $200,000. But it was still one of the least-expensive McLarens.

CHAPTER 4

ULTIMATE SERIES

McLaren's fastest cars were in the Ultimate Series. The McLaren P1 replaced the F1 in the 2010s. Then the W1 came in the 2020s. It added an even stronger engine.

The McLaren P1 had a lower top speed than the F1. But it could hit high speeds more quickly.

The Senna came out in 2017. It became McLaren's fastest track car.

    The McLaren Senna had an extreme, sporty design. The cabin had many windows. They gave drivers a 180-degree view.

FAST FACT
The Senna was named after Ayrton Senna. He was a Formula 1 driver.

The McLaren Speedtail had a top speed of 250 miles per hour (403 km/h).

McLaren Speedtails had low tails that could bend. These features helped lower **drag** and keep the cars steady. McLaren continued to satisfy fans who had a need for speed.

Solus GT

The Solus GT had just one seat. Its huge fins and air vents looked unlike any other car's. Each Solus GT sold for more than $3 million.

McLaren made only 25 Solus GTs.

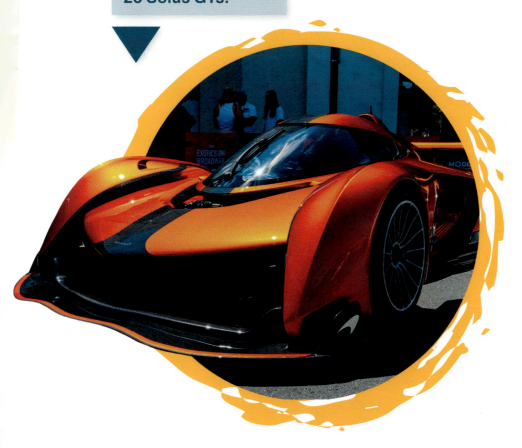

COMPREHENSION QUESTIONS

Write your answers on a separate piece of paper.

1. Write a few sentences explaining the main ideas of Chapter 2.

2. Which McLaren model would you most like to have? Why?

3. When was McLaren founded?
    - **A.** 1963
    - **B.** 1974
    - **C.** 1992

4. What is McLaren named after?
    - **A.** a famous racetrack
    - **B.** the company's fastest car
    - **C.** the company's founder

5. What does **veers** mean in this book?

*Norris **veers** around a tight turn.*

    A. moves straight
    B. changes direction
    C. stops moving

6. What does **dominant** mean in this book?

*Norris stays in front from start to finish. His **dominant** race helps his team win the Constructor's Championship!*

    A. very difficult
    B. very unlucky
    C. very successful

Answer key on page 32.

GLOSSARY

brand
The products and services connected with one company.

designed
Planned how to make or build something.

drag
The force of air or water pushing back against a moving object.

exhausts
Systems that let out used gases from cars.

Formula 1
The highest level of open-wheel racing.

Grand Prix
A car race on a difficult course that is part of a world championship series.

hybrid
A machine that can use two different sources of energy, such as gas and electricity.

intakes
Parts that let things in.

BOOKS

Duling, Kaitlyn. *McLaren 750S*. Bellwether Media, 2025.

Orr, Tamra. *McLaren GT*. Kaleidoscope, 2022.

Rains, Dalton. *Formula 1 Racing*. Apex Editions, 2024.

ONLINE RESOURCES

Visit **www.apexeditions.com** to find links and resources related to this title.

ABOUT THE AUTHOR

Dalton Rains is a writer and editor from St. Paul, Minnesota. He would love to drive a McLaren someday.

INDEX

#
750S, 18
765LT, 19

A
Abu Dhabi Grand Prix, 4, 7–8
Artura, 16, 18

C
carbon fiber, 13
Constructor's Championship, 8, 12

F
F1, 15, 22
Formula 1, 4, 7–8, 10, 13, 25

G
GTS, 20

M
McLaren, Bruce, 10, 12
MP4/1, 13

N
Norris, Lando, 4, 7–8

P
P1, 22

S
Senna, 24–25
Senna, Ayrton, 25
Solus GT, 27
Speedtails, 26

W
W1, 22

ANSWER KEY:
1. Answers will vary; 2. Answers will vary; 3. A; 4. C; 5. B; 6. C

32